Small Towns And Mountain Views

Zualteii Poonte

BlueRose ONE .com
Stories Matter
New Delhi • London

BLUEROSE PUBLISHERS
India | U.K.

For permissions requests or inquiries regarding this publication, please contact:

BLUEROSE PUBLISHERS
www.BlueRoseONE.com
info@bluerosepublishers.com
+91 8882 898 898
+4407342408967

ISBN: 978-93-7542-331-7

Cover Design: Deepak Katheria
Typesetting: Manisha Rawat

First Edition: March 2026

Dedication

To my parents,
Bonthanga Poonte (1930-1975) and K. Thanchhingi (1933-1994)
for your encouragement since those Mr. Grumpy days.
Thank you for everything

Acknowledgements

Some poems and prose pieces in this book have earlier appeared in the following publications -

The Poetry of SOUL, USA, 2015: "The Fog," "January", "The Unwinding", "Put Away", "Last Night I Heard the Wind Outside", "Morning Pools of the Sky People", "Anatomy of a Big, Black Rainstorm in the Mountains", and "Against the Wind"

Journal of MIELS, 2015: "Put Away"

Journal of Literature and Cultural Studies, 2016: "The Slip Away" and "December"

Amarvati Poetic Prism, 2016: "Last Night I Heard the Wind Outside"

Prose Writings from North East India, 2021: "Anatomy of a Big, Black Rainstorm on the Mountains"

The Keepers of Knowledge: Writings from Mizoram, 2023: "September", "October" and "December"

YMA newsletter, June 2025: "June"

A huge thank you to VL Hruaitluanga for permission to use your superb drone shot of Aizawl for my book cover.

My most profound and sincere thank you to Easterine Kire for your generous support and encouragement in bringing out this book. I would have given up without you, truly.

Also to Malsawmi Jacob for your kind advice and guidance in going through my manuscript in its very early stages.

Mona Zote for having a look at my early manuscript, and the emphatic advice to throw out some things which will remain unmentioned here!

Somte Ralte for generously sharing your publishing experiences and know-how.

To my sisters, Mapuii and Peggy, and Hmingpuii and her family.

And to all my fellow Mizo writers in English.

Contents

Poetry

The Fog

And it comes again
this fog
stealing in silently
clouding over in slow degrees
all that was crystal clear,
like the fog in my mind does
sometimes.

The Unwinding

A woman's muted laugh,
a male voice, drunken, loud,
uncaring of the time of night.
"Shhh, shhhhhh!"
"WHAT, IT'S EARLY YET, NOT SLEEPING TIME"

Away in the distance a dog barks,
a lone bike roars,
a truck rumbles,
a window pulls shut.
The dog on the couch sighs
in its sleep,
on the bedside table
tick tick tick tock.

Day unravels, dissolves quietly
in the dark.

Closures

Rivers can't hold onto their waters
though the waters be with the river a while,
banked in, held gently,
sharing sun and rain,
soon the waters must
move on to find
their places in the sea,
and the river must embrace a new flow of waters
because rivers can't hold onto their waters
though the waters be with the river a while.

Last Night I Heard the Wind Outside

Last night I heard the wind outside
struggling to break
free from the trees.
It stretched and pulled at
branches and leaves that
wouldn't let go,
and snarled and howled
for freedom.
This morning, all around me I see
scattered debris
of its profitless fury
vented on twigs and
new-born Mayflowers
trampled and crushed in the rain.

The trees today stand
unmoving and silent
and the wind, like a
beaten adversary,
subdued and stilled
within them.
Perhaps it's at rest
in the roots
of the trees
like the spirits my ancestors
once propitiated.*

**Early Mizos believed that spirits inhabited large rocks and tree roots, and sacrifices, such as poultry, were offered to appease them*

The Slip Away

When it comes
at a time when life
no longer holds promise or magic,
when ailments are part of daily life,
and you no longer dream dreams
for so many have been realised,
you feel you shouldn't be too greedy
but be satisfied with what you have,
and your discontent with what you are
and what you have accomplished
is quietly washed away with drink.

But the drink eats away at you,
at your insides, and time after time
you cheat death
in painful, close escapes,
and you go on,
tiredly,
knowing you're not too old yet to sit back on life
while all too aware you're no longer
young enough to start afresh
and tackle those dreams you never fulfilled.

That's when it comes,
the swift, sudden call,
and you go, quietly, alone,
you let go for it seems so easy
to slip away from the weariness of it all
and you don't really care anymore
what waits on the other side.

Misfits

Mid-forties, single and childless
you attend a Church Women service
but all they seem to talk about is
caring for your husband and kids.

Mid-thirties, well-settled in a career
you attend a Christian Youth conference
but all the Speaker talks about is
studying hard so you succeed in life.

Mid-teens, a school dropout
you attend Sunday School
but all the teachers talk about is
how you must work hard at school.

A young love-child living with
a single mother or grandparents,
all you ever hear anywhere is
how you must love and obey your parents.

In a society built on black and white constructs,
where do we shades of grey fit in?

Put Away

(for Zokunga, 1925 – 1966)

The dreaded rapping on the door after dark
Just a little talk with him outside we want
The wanted gets up, steps out the house
Be back soon, you all go to sleep
But he never does.
Sometimes if they're lucky
they find the body a short distance down the road.
More often deep in the jungle they find it
in a shallow grave
sometimes marked, sometimes not.

My mother's brother's body was never found,
He disappeared without trace,
wiped off the face of the earth,
not a limb, not a nail, not a hair left to claim.
Almost half a century on,
still no one to come forward and say
*Here, those are pearls that were his eyes.**

Nothing for the left behind,
parents, brothers, sisters, wife,
his brood of nine young children.
Nothing.
Nothing.
Just the incomprehensible, unceasing uncertainty
of questions never answered.

The title is a literal translation of the MNF terminology "dah tha/ dah that," an insidious euphemism meaning killed/murdered/exterminated.

**There were unverified reports later that my uncle had been shot dead at Tlawng river by rebels who were later killed in turn by soldiers of the Indian Army.*

The Silence of Sundays

One day, some day,
when the pandemic is over
and the world is back to normal
I will look back and miss
the quiet of Sundays:
the stillness, the peace,
the leisurely calm,
the streets silent and emptied
of traffic and pedestrians
but for the odd two-wheeler or two
running an emergency.
The Sundays that kept us at home
from church, our social meetings,
the bells clanging at 10
in reminder of busier times.

For now, I will bask
in the soothing winter sunshine
and soak in this quietude.

Of Time and a Classroom Table

How many young people have sat here
through the years
patiently listening to countless confusing lectures,
or losing the battle against heavy eyelids
as a teacher drones on
on a sweltering summer's day,
or in the back row carrying on a whispered conversation
with a friend under cover of an open textbook
propped up on the table,
or struggling through an exam
to earn that coveted degree.

Where are they now, those generations of young learners,
who have moved on to take their places in the world -
some clergymen with flocks to lead to heavenly destinations,
politicians, officers, media persons, entrepreneurs, educators,
some in distant, far-flung villages,
some dead and at slumber beneath the earth,
some fathers and mothers with offspring of their own
coming to sit at these very same tables.

This old table, once smooth and new, gleaming with fresh paint,
now decrepit and battered, scarred with scratches,
and marked with memories of people and time.

We Are Nostalgia

(for the Chhuahtlang people)

We are nostalgia
old friends who go back a long, long way,
raw-boned and scrawny,
barely out of our teens,
a motley bunch
in pursuit of a master's degree
in that cold, pine-needled land across the state
because ours didn't have
a postgraduate setup then.

Coping with study stress, cultural divides
and bouts of homesickness,
we sealed strong bonds at *Mayurbhanj*[1], *Long View*[2], and *Bijni*[3],
over guitar sing-alongs, dinners, socials, and picnics
out in the wilds where the boys would disappear
into the bushes (for Dutch courage)
before asking the girls for a dance,
and complain when the girls wouldn't oblige
but declare it time to get back to the hostel.

Vacation time, homeward bound,
early morning risings to catch the hired bus,
long hours on winding mountain roads,
stopping for meals at little shacks,
rewinding cassette reels with a ball pen,
nodding off on one another's shoulders,
promises to stay in touch.

Forty odd years later,
no longer young or starry-eyed
but retired and content in having left imprints
in our own ways,
old friends now meet at funerals, gathering for
photographs
over wood coffins as death stakes claim on us, one by one,
and at condolence meets with family
we reminisce fondly on those good old days.

So much history forged together,
yes, my friend, we are nostalgia.

[1] *Mayurbhanj: campus of the North Eastern Hill University, Shillong, in the 1980s*
[2] *Long View: one of the NEHU boys' hostels*

[3] *Bijni: NEHU girls' hostel*

A Month in the Life of a Head of Department

April is the cruellest month
dredging up paperwork for the exams next month,
crunching the number of classes attended this semester
or not, as the case may be.

Miss, I was away for two months on college duty
for sports practice,
or lit club tour of heritage places,
or climbing mountains with the adventure club
or at cadet fall-ins and training camps.
Here's our attendance records, miss.

Sigh, do you kids come here to be educated
or play sports, climb walls and perform drills anyway?
Cooking your attendance records is not
my idea of a clear conscience but
I don't expect you to understand that.

Just let me sit for the exams, Miss, give me a chance
I'll be a model student next time, I promise.
Wait, you didn't submit an assignment paper
or turn up for your internal tests.

Miss, I was sick, nobody told me, I didn't understand the topic
Right, you didn't understand but four hundred
of your classmates did and turned in papers
by the sheaves that we slogged over
till you all had little numbers to your names
added to the cooked attendance figures
so that next month you can sit for exams
you'll probably only study for the night before!

Dear Easterine

Dear Easterine,
Every time I pick up your book of poetry
it reminds me of a little jewel box -
the gleaming gems nestling inside,
some small and fragmentary but all
honed and polished to perfection
by a master craftsman.

The iridescent moonstone of your mother's earthleavingness
that echoes mine so painfully,
the diamond hellos to old friends - the wind and rain,
fog and moonlight, and childhood memories..
the glittering amethyst purple rain in April
from the Windhover Collection you once
told me is your favourite book..
the tinkle of goat-bells in the emerald grass,
the lapis lazuli of earthbound clouds
and the little pearl cloud-dog which went away
to live in heaven with Jesus and his decibels.

I will hold this little treasure chest close to my heart,
rifling through it oftentimes till every jewel
feels like a dearly loved friend.

The Railway Tourists

They come in hordes
of coach-loads from the new railroad line
that opened us up one overcast September day.

And they surge in, curious to see
this insular hill state they know not of
apart from social media -
the Silent City vlogs and reels,
sweeping images of emerald green mountains
and valleys awash with clouds,
houses upon houses perilously perched on cliffsides,
the diamond lights by night.

Yes, our land is beautiful
and they love it too.
The bracing air, nature untouched,
the locals who do not speak Hindi,
unapologetically Christian,
the different culture, different food,
they lap it all up,
happily chasing sunrise and sunsets
over frothy foaming clouds.

Once in the 80s
when none had heard of us,
on a college excursion at Juhu beach,
locals asked where we were from.
"Mizoram," a friend said, and one of them
asked, "uh, near Mexico?"

Now they know we're just
one railroad junction away.

Calendar Poems

January

Chilly mornings
wrapped in fog,
the leaves on the trees
shiver,
the sad wintry sun
cannot break through
the greyed-out landscape.
Inside the house
echoes bounce off white, naked walls
stripped of Christmas trimmings.

Hello again, January,
to you I raise a gently steaming
cup of tea.

February

I felt a poem stir in me today
at the day's dull opening
of shrouded sunrise and overcast skies.
February's on the wing and
summer's warm breath stealing in
But this cheerless morning felt like
winter wasn't letting go until the sun
burst through and all was sunny and light again
but my little poem died in the rushing around
of washing clothes and hanging them to dry
and a hundred other sunny day chores.

At 9 tonight, rain rattled down the tin roof
and my poem came back to life
so now I'm warmly tucked in bed
tapping out these cold day in February blues.

March

March of the dry and dust, gusts of wind
blow away winter's last remains
bringing in summer's hot breath.

A dimming memory of a long-ago day
the family fleeing Aizawl in fear
into the mountains
the plane that roared overhead
looking for people to drop bombs on.
March today is less traumatic:
blackened ash flakes swirl in bright sunlight,
spring showers water the parched earth,
the old and the young get drunk on
the spirit of *Chapchar Kut**.

And the year marches on.

**Chapchar Kut: the Mizo spring festival*

April

Eliot was right when he wrote
that April is the cruellest month
and had he lived in these parts
he would have meant the heat
that explodes in the dry brittle air,
the windows that stay open by night
and waken you time and again
to the next door child crying
or the parents squabbling in raised tones.

April showers come suddenly
in short, sharp gushes, bringing moments
of sweet relief but as quickly as the wet dries,
the heat returns blinding and muggy.
Fruits ripen, flowers colour the earth,
jacarandas grace the landscape in fresh mauve.

Summer is here in full, fine throttle.

May

A quiet Sunday,
May is running out of days
The *gulmohar** flaunts scarlet remnants of its flowers,
the ones left untouched by rain,
a little bird sings before the mist rolls in
and the afternoon shower comes.

A hot cup of evening tea,
you call a friend on the phone
but she doesn't answer.
Cup in hand, you sit by the window
and watch the sun's last rays
light up trees in the distance
entangled in white wisps of fog.

* *Royal Poinciana tree, also known as Delonix Regia or the Mayflower tree. April par in Mizo*

June

Mid-June, mid-monsoon,
raindrops cluster on windows,
tree branches sway in the wind outside.

The front page of *Vanglaini*[1] this morning carries
a picture of workers in a clearing on a steep hillside,
bent low and weeding,
The caption says the YMA[2] of Samthang village yesterday
came together to weed the land of a farmer
ailing and unable to tend to his land.

The paper also says there were 83 volunteers in all.
Perhaps the man has cancer, the paper doesn't say
but it moves me to tears.

Through rapidly changing values and priorities
Tlawmngaihna[3] lives on,
and my faith in humanity restored
this dismal monsoonal day.

[1] *Vanglaini: the widest-selling daily newspaper in Mizoram*
[2] *YMA: Young Mizo Association, the largest secular, non-government group in the state*
[3] *Tlawmngaihna: a Mizo code of conduct alluding to altruism, selflessness, or a strong sense of duty and service to others*

July

Two Julys, and forty years in between..

A shy 21 year old steps into a classroom,
timid and unsure, tasked with the challenge
to instill English and literature in students
whose mother tongue it is not.

Forty Julys later, a seasoned teacher retires,
tired but happy to have helped mould
so many young minds to make
their own July imprints on the world.

The in-between of those two Julys
encapsulate my productive years.
My days of sun, of rain, of clouds,
of growth and evolution -
Label me *"Made in July."*

August

August with its
wild, sweeping curtains of fog and mist
that cover and lift, and cover and lift
over the landscape throughout the day.

And the rain,
the relentless, unceasing rain
that pounds and punishes the earth;
the sludge on roads
of mud from hillsides that slide
in slow motion, dislodging
full grown trees left rootless
in brutal aftermath.

And when the rains hold,
the heavy humid heat that
oppresses and threatens
yet more rain.

The rain reigns most days in August.

September

September is
the monsoon on its way out and sulking,
casting breaths of impenetrable grey fog across the landscape,
a nip in the air, forecasting
heavy woollens, shorter days and longer nights.

September is
rain that splatters summer dust on the streets
into a gooey mush *Beihrual**-goers
gingerly skirt around in the early-darkened evenings.

September is
the month my sister turned four,
Grandma's birthday party for her abandoned
with a messenger bringing news
of Father's death in hospital.

September is
coming home from school on a cold, wet afternoon,
Mother prone on the bed, weeping with abandon
into the blankets,
my sister beside her, quiet with bewilderment.
I never saw Mother cry so hard,
with so much pain, it frightened me,
I never mentioned Father's name in her presence again,
Neither did my sisters for reasons of their own.

Years later she would ask
"Why do you never speak of your father?"

September.

**Beihrual: Evening services in Mizoram held in the month of September not in church but in private homes. It commemorates the early days when believers would hold devotional services in the homes of church members to reaffirm and strengthen their faith*

October

And suddenly it's October again.
The dank dark damp will soon be gone
with the slush and wet. Shadows
will lengthen in the angled sunlight
we shall warm our backs to
on chilly mornings when winter sets in.

Morning pools of cotton wool
white-wreathed across valleys and mountains,
blue skies piled with immense white clouds,
evenings that explode with colour,
brown confetti from the *gulmohar* tree
long past its May days of glory.

The dry and dust bring back childhood memories,
riding homeward from sun-baked plains
up cool, winding highland roads
the nuns at boarding school left far behind,
Dad wrapping a warm arm around one of us,
home to Mum and the dear little house
at the top of the dusty hill.

Season changes worm out memories
buried in time. And the more things change,
the more things remain the same.

November

My birth month.
My mother and grandmother spoke often of how
Mother almost died giving birth to me.
A home birth, grandma the midwife.

Mother had an easy time with her firstborn
the previous year; with me it was different.
Shortly after I was born Mother began
fading away, slipping into unconsciousness,
In the panic that ensued, Grandma grabbed
a lit tobacco roll, held it to Mother's mouth
and screamed, "Inhale, inhale, inhale!"
Mother's lungs kicked in with the deep breaths
pulling her back from the darkness.
She lived and so did I.

But it always made me feel a little guilty
that I had almost killed her, if unknowingly.

December

December,
and they come in droves -
some for Christmas shopping
with money they've saved all year,
some to see the big city
they've heard of all their lives,
some persuaded finally to see the doctors
for that nagging stomach discomfort
they've been putting on hold
through the long, hard months
of slash and burn, sowing and weeding
and finally the harvest,
all under the burning sun
and pouring rains.

Some are easy to tell -
lean, skeletal almost,
sunbrowned, clothed in sombre colours,
together in groups of threes or fours,
clearly not at ease
in the jostling throng on the streets.
Others, while also from the provinces,
but spared perhaps the more brutal agrarian labour,
blend in more easily with the city crowd
of smooth faced young girls strolling in pairs,
identical in fur lined boots and slim fit clothing,
sweet-smelling young boys,
jackets zipped up to the chin,
swinging bike helmets in leather gloved hands,
children clutching plastic toys from China,
licking ice cream, as weary parents in tow
pause at mounds of secondhand winterwear

piled high on each corner of every street,
patient women fruit sellers
with neat stacks of sweet, juicy oranges,
*Red Kettle volunteers** grouped
at strategic intersections,
breaking into loud, brassy snatches
of well-loved carols.

It's Christmas time in the city,
fast paced and frenetic.
Soon they'll rattle back to the villages
on roads baked passable in the dry season,
and exhaustedly, they will exclaim,
"How crowded Aizawl is,
how can anyone even stand to live there!"

**Red Kettle volunteers: Salvation Army volunteers for the Red Kettle campaign to raise money for various projects especially at Christmas time*

Prose

Morning Pools of the Sky People

It happens late in the year every year, around the time when the rains taper off and the harvests in the rice fields begin to ripen and glow golden in the sun. From the wee hours past midnight when earth people are in bed in blissful slumber, the fabled *van mi* or sky people leave their homes in the sky to stealthily descend to earth for a few joyous hours of bathing and swimming.

Under the pale light of the moon, between mountains and high hills, they create huge pools of spray and water that is so pure and white it looks like soft, downy cotton wool. The pools cover entire valleys, stretching from one far distance to another, running up the sides of mountains and creating occasional happy little islands in the middle. Some pools sweep across vast expanses like tumultuous, turgid seas while others are sandwiched between mountains and towns like hungry rivers. In the bewitched pools, the sky people play and gambol and frolic to their heart's content. Sometimes they take gravity-defying dives off cliffs or jump from trees into the surging white waters.

Then as the sun awakens and unhurriedly rises, lazily stretching out its brilliant rays over the mountain tops, the sky people sigh and begin to gather their things to go back to their homes in the sky. A few dawdlers, reluctant to leave the water, linger on but as the sun gets stronger and the earth gets warmer, the waters in the enchanted pools dissipate slowly till there is nothing left but empty air and mist. One by one, the lingerers too return to their homes. The pools remain amidst the mountains and rills for a while as earth people wake up and rub their eyes in marvel at the sight outside. By the time the clocks on the earth people's walls point to eight, the pools have mostly all disappeared. Late risers who are excitedly told about the magical pools thrust their necks out of windows but see nothing but green valleys and hills.

Of Dusk and Swings

And if light shall fade
and fall to black...

There's probably some psychology term for it but a certain memory comes to mind every time I watch dusk fall - which isn't every day with all the things happening at the end of the day that prevent you from just sitting back and watching the world changing outside. I also happen to live on the eastern side of a hill which means I get to watch sunrises but sunsets never.

But I digress. Dusk somehow always brings back to mind a particular image. A little girl sitting on a swing, all on her own while nature shifts and changes colours all around her. I was about 9 or 10, recently sent off to a boarding school called St. Agnes Convent in the small, idyllic town of Haflong in Assam (albeit with my two sisters) after years of living with my grandparents. The school had two sections separated from each other by a large, grassy field with a narrow, cobbled pathway connecting the two sections. One section housed the classrooms, and the other was the main, rambling, Assam type building with dormitories for the boarders and a closed off section housing the chapel and nuns.

The swings were in the classroom section and were always in great demand during lunch breaks and before classes in the morning. I never even dreamed of trying to get a turn at those times. Instead, sometimes in the evenings when the pushy day-scholars had gone home and the hostel girls were all busy doing something or the other, I would wend my way alone down the cobbled path and have the swings all to myself. There were two of them, built side by side - one was high and scary and the big girls loved to ride on it, giggling and screaming. The other one was child sized. I would sit on the wooden seat of the smaller one and swing to my heart's content. Everything would be peaceful and quiet except for a few crickets singing in the trees and hedges. I would listen to the swing's iron hinges creak as dusk fell around me. The world would grow soft and mellow, enveloped in swift changing hues of crimson, pink, orange and purple and I would think of how the older girls always talked about how homesick they felt at sundown. Maybe I was too young to feel homesick, or maybe since I had never really lived with my parents since preschool age, I was never particularly heartsick. But I did sense something sad and lingering in the air around me. And then I would remember the classrooms behind me were supposed to be haunted so I would get up and make my way back to the dormitory before it got too dark.

Anatomy of a Big, Black Rainstorm on the Mountains

Ruahthimpui is what we call them up here in these highlands. *Ruah* for rain, *thim* for dark, *pui* for big, so literally a big, black rainstorm. As opposed to those summery showers which thoroughly wet your umbrella but don't last very long.

Early Mizos, well attuned to the vagaries of nature and remarkably observant despite lack of formal education, noted and named different kinds of rains throughout the year. Such as the *pawl delh ruah* (literally paddy straw flattening rain) which comes in late December or early January and flattens the paddy straw left in the fields after the harvests; the *to ruah* (growth/spring rain) in March which helps vegetation spring back to life after the dry season; the *nikir ruah* (summer solstice rain) which arrives quite punctually around the 20th of June and lasts an entire wet, miserable week; the *ruah phingphisiau,* a very light drizzle common in July; the *ruah mual liam* (a kind of spot rain which pours down on a concentrated area and quickly moves on) which comes mostly in August and September; the *ai ruah,* a three day rain that shows up in late October or early November and announces the beginning of autumn, etc.

A *ruahthimpui* usually visits these high mountains in Mizoram sometimes unexpectedly at the beginning of the year around early March, much before the onset of the monsoon rains, and more usually in early May.

There's never really any indication earlier on in the day that a *ruahthimpui* is brewing. No bleary sunrise, no overcast skies, no agitated bird alarms. Just business as usual everywhere, people going about their work, children playing outside. Then suddenly, thick dark clouds start sweeping ominously down the mountains, a strong wind whips out of nowhere and noisily flaps clothes hanging out on lines, bangs shut unbolted windows and doors, stirs dust from the ground and sends debris swirling in the air. There are short, sharp sounds everywhere. Glass shattering, neighbours calling out to one another in high, hurried tones as they rush around collecting their wash, voices screaming for the children to get indoors immediately. Windows and doors are hastily shut and firmly bolted, rolling shutters of shop doors noisily dragged way down low, people on the streets, with or without umbrellas, rush for the nearest shelter. Lightning streaks viciously across blackened skies and thunder rumbles.

Within minutes, heavy raindrops smack fatly down, relentlessly rattling tin rooftops and glass windows. A smothering curtain of grey, impenetrable mist and fog settles over everything, drawing visibility to claustrophobic limits. Sometimes, little ice balls of petrified rain pelt down, hammering car tops and tin-roofed houses. Hail always causes excitement. Children are especially fascinated and a few daring ones dart outside to pick up the glistening, white stones.

Within four walls, the electricity is invariably cut off. Darkness reigns supreme. People light candles or old-fashioned lanterns at noon, a few awestruck faces peer through glass panes at nature's unleashed fury raging outside. Some huddle down on long chairs, others bunk down under warm blankets in bed to comfortably wait out the storm.

Sometimes it continues for as long as almost an hour. Sometimes it's done in a few minutes. The rain stops, the fog clears, the clouds roll back to their places somewhere beyond the mountains. The sun reappears. People open windows and doors and come outside. Everything is bedraggled and dripping. And life picks up again.

Two Exhumations and a Re-interment

After time gaps of 43 and 30 years respectively, in 2013, both my maternal grandparents were re-interred.

One September evening in 1969, my grandfather had been struck down by a speeding car and killed. Like many families in Aizawl, Mizoram's capital, ours had fled in the terror-filled days of the *rambuai* in 1966 and settled down in Shillong where I started schooling, with my two sisters and two cousins. Grandma lived with us while my parents went back to Mizoram. Grandpa divided his time between Shillong and Aizawl. That fatal September, he was in Shillong with some Mizo church leaders for the opening of a Mizo Church, and they were all walking home when the car sped by. The other men managed to jump out of the way but not my grandfather. He was already 74 and obviously not as agile as the others. The car knocked him down flat and raced away, and was never traced: it left Grandma a widow.

It was a time when all journeys were taken by road, and with the *rambuai* problem, vehicles had to travel in convoys, with stopovers and sleepovers enroute. Since some of the family, including Grandma, were already living in Shillong, it was decided that it would be easier to bury him there. And so on the slope of a little pine hill in *Laitumkhrah*[1] cemetery, Grandpa was laid to rest.

A few years later, the family, including my grandmother, moved back to Aizawl, to the family home at *Mission Veng*[2]. In 1976, she suffered a sudden stroke which left her paralyzed on the entire left side of her body. She managed to survive that until 1982 when she broke her left thigh bone in a fall. She was then living with my family at *Chanmari*[3]. Her health declined rapidly and in July, she passed on to join my grandfather. She was buried at the Chanmari cemetery.

Several years later in 2013, following faintly hoped-for but never actuated family dreams, it was decided that Grandpa's bones be brought back home and reburied at the Mission Veng cemetery. And since most of our extended family live at Mission Veng anyway, Grandmother's bones should also be brought to join her husband in his final resting place.

And so it was that both my grandparents' bones were re-laid to rest in a little white satin-covered coffin. Three senior male members of the family travelled to Shillong to locate Grandfather's grave and reopen it. His remains, as scanty as might be expected after 43 long years, were reverently gathered and brought back home. Meanwhile, back home in Aizawl, some of us worked on exhuming Grandma's grave for her remains. It was an experience that made me realise how insubstantial human life is. Once we die, we pass into nothingness, our carrion passing back into the earth. Ashes to ashes, dust to dust. All is vanity.

My grandfather, Pu Zalawra, is today an established name in Mizo Church history, most notably in connection with the Sunday School that he had helped set up. My grandmother, Pi Lalnemi, was just an ordinary, extraordinary woman who took good care of her family. They lived and they died; their mortal remains today mere debris. But they live on in and through their descendants and so long as we live, they will too.

Rest in peace, Grandma and Grandpa.

[1]*Laitumkhrah – one of the oldest and most well-established neighbourhoods in Shillong*

[2]*Mission Veng – one of the oldest and most well-established neighbourhoods in Aizawl*

[3]*Chandmari – another well-established neighbourhood in Aizawl*

Of Convoys and Road Journeys

It's late at night or in the very early hours of the morning that it happens. When the hubbub of the world is stilled, and all is silent as people rest tired bodies and lose themselves to dreams and deep slumber. It's not even something that I experience very often, being a sound sleeper. But once in a while, something awakens me and in the brief moments of wakefulness, I hear it. The distant rumble of a truck, the thrum of its engine or the long low honk of a truck horn as it wends its way along some road somewhere. Memories steal in, now mere fragments with the onslaught of time but vivid in their tenacity.

Long queues of trucks parked along a winding road in darkness. Military trucks, Bedford lorries, the odd jeep or two, an *Assam State Transport bus*[1] with its distinctive rhino symbol. As the trucks grind to a tired halt, my mind replays the sound I recall so well even these decades upon decades later – a sibilant hiss as compressed air from miles of driving over rough mountain terrain is released from the brakes. The handyman jumping smartly down from the elevated truck cabin to deftly place a wooden wedge against a rear wheel so the truck does not roll away. Passengers moving about quietly, stretching legs and backs after being cooped up inside the vehicles for hours, some making for nearby bushes in urgent answer to nature's call.

In those difficult times, military escort parties shepherded all vehicles moving around the territory laden with essential supplies and passengers, both military and civil. Convoy Commanders, usually young army captains, assigned to provide safe passage against insurgent ambushes, empowered to make stops and starts for the thirty to forty strong vehicle convoy and authorised to take any necessary action in the event of trouble. With nighttime journeys obviously unthinkable, the convoy Commander would call for a night halt at day's end and military personnel would unload provisions of water and rice bags and cook evening meals on kerosene stoves by the roadside. Most passengers carried their own tiffins, as they called them, while the army men would share their food with those with nothing to eat. Since I was a little too young to remember details, an older cousin with a sharper memory tells me that my grandmother would carry boiled eggs, potatoes and rice that she had laboriously prepared in advance to feed her little family enroute the long journey. Once the meals were eaten and cleared, passengers would get back to their respective vehicles for an uneasy, restless night's sleep in cargo holds sheathed with thick waterproof tarpaulin. The next morning, after quick obligatory revisits to the nearby bushes, the truck engines would throb back to life and the convoy would be on the move once again. Another convoy traveller tells me that there was no washing of faces or brushing of teeth, unless there was a little stream nearby, no morning tea or meal, none of which particularly bothered poverty-hardened survivors of a famine which had directly caused the *rambuai*[2].

But it's not just convoy memories that nocturnal motor sounds evoke. For years the only passage for Mizos to the rest of the world was via the *Silchar*[3] route, now part of the Indian National Highway 54. A tortuously winding road snaking through the mountains with a steep fall on one side and cliff slopes overgrown with vegetation on the other, just barely wide enough for two heavy vehicles to pass each other. Landslides were common occurrences particularly during the rainy season, causing time-consuming delays and forcing travellers to sometimes spend several days in covering the slightly less than 200-kilometre distance between Aizawl and Silchar.

Having travelled up and down this highway several times in my early years, first for survival and refuge, and later for schooling in Shillong, *Haflong*[4] and Darjeeling, I remember how fresh and bracing the mountain air felt especially when returning home from the scorching plains of Silchar. But the physical passage through it was often difficult and challenging. At times when the road was impassable due to landslides and rockfalls, travellers had to make do with spending nights either snatching naps in the buses, cars or jeeps, or taking grateful shelter in one of the little villages along the way, the inhabitants of which were used to unexpected overnight guests.

The shadow of rebel ambushes and attacks along travel routes persisted long after the rigid convoy travel restrictions for civilians had eased off. On one occasion, this time at the height of summer in June 1980, I was part of a college excursion tour visiting various cities in the country – Calcutta, Bombay (as they were then known) and Delhi where the first thing we did, after freshening up from the long train journey from Gauhati, was to visit Pu Laldenga, leader of the MNF, at the insistence of the boys in our tour party. He was then living in Delhi for peace negotiations with the Central Government, and as we all crowded into their sitting room, the boys hung on to his every word in hushed reverence as he spoke persuasively about politics in low, confidential tones, while most of the girls dozed off in exhaustion.

By the end of the tour, we finally headed home, piling onto our hired Mizoram State Transport Bus at Silchar, relieved to leave behind the heat of the plains and breathe in refreshing cool air. We happily sang songs (as Mizos tend to do when riding long distance in vehicles) – patriotic Mizo songs, Christian songs, and the bus sailed past the small border towns of Vairengte and Bilkhawthlir without incident. At the outskirts of the next town, Kolasib, we were stopped to be told that MNF rebels had ambushed an Indian Army bus, killing four and injuring others, literally minutes after we had driven past. One of the boys remarked that the rebels had probably already been in position, hiding and waiting in the bushes by the road, and seen and heard us singing as we moved past. It was an unsettling thought.

I recall that it was also on this occasion that the bus was stopped once more, this time because there had been an accident, of which there were regrettably many, given the treacherous terrain. A truck had driven off the road and a rescue effort was underway for the victims. As we got off the bus to stretch our legs, a team of rescue volunteers were just climbing out of the ravine with one of the bodies – a smallish figure, a woman we were told, slackened in death, and respectfully laid by the roadside, shrouded in a Mizo *puan*[5]. Mizos are reverential with their dead, with a "mitthi puan" traditionally brought by mourners to drape over the mortal remains of the departed soul by way of paying their last respects. In case of accidents in isolated places, such as road accidents, at least one or two women who happen to be nearby quickly remove their puan to cover the body. Or when *YMA*[6] rescue teams set out in search of missing persons, many volunteers carry along a puan in case the missing is found dead.

It's been many years since but I remember all too well the sound and feel of sitting in a vehicle lumbering along the mountain roads, swaying and lurching past kilometre after kilometre of thick jungles and little highway hamlets. The steady hum of the engine gently lulling passengers into exhausted sleep, woven into which were the frequent honks of the motor as it navigated countless twists and turns through the winding road, while manoeuvring past the many goods trucks coming from Silchar, heavy-laden with provisions for the Mizo populace.

In retrospect, I suppose having spent so much of my early life on those long road journeys, I will always retain a great deal of nostalgia for sights and sounds that remind me of those days, no matter how traumatic or exhausting. And nighttime sounds will continue to wake me from time to time, bringing in whispers of those long gone, long done, long ago yesterdays.

[1]*Assam State Transport*: Mizoram was earlier part of the state of Assam and called the Mizo Hills District before becoming the Union Territory of Mizoram in 1972 and achieving full statehood in 1987

[2]*rambuai* - the Mizo Uprising/ Revolt (known as the *buai* or *rambuai* in Mizo) led by the Mizo National Front (MNF) which broke out on March the 6th 1966 with a declaration of independence from the Indian government, a direct consequence of the Mautam famine of 1960 when the Indian govt. did little to help the Mizo people

[3] *Silchar* - a small town in Assam

[4] *Haflong* – a small town and hill station in Assam

[5] *puan* – traditional attire for Mizo women, a sarong-like cloth wrapped around the waist and covering the legs

[6] *YMA* – Young Mizo Association, the largest secular, non-government group in the state

Of Spring Rains

Ṭo ruah a haw. The spring rains have come.

Surely these must be among the most anticipated words since time immemorial. At least in these parts. Winter is so dry. The skies shut off from October except for occasional random downpours, until the sun progressively scorches to turn everything dry and sere. Sand and grit everywhere. Then there are the inevitable ash flakes that float lazily through the air from the *jhum* fields to settle on our pristinely clean floors through open doors and windows. Whirling round and round with the help of the mad March winds. Rivulets and streams dry up. Water supply becomes erratic. We scratch dry skins and pray for rain.

And then it comes. Sometime after midnight, it comes splattering down, waking you from your restless dreams. *Ṭo ruah a haw e.*

My First Memory

What is your first memory? This was a question on one of those timepass games that came up on my Facebook page a few years ago. I had reflected for a minute, then quickly typed out a gist of the following without giving it much thought. Later I was surprised to see shocked reactions from friends, including a thoughtful comment that said no wonder it was my first memory because it must have been so traumatic. I had never really thought of it as traumatic but looking back, I can see why it stood out.

The first memory I have is of fleeing home during the *rambuai*. Early 1966. I was all of three years and three months old. Mother, sisters, grandparents, aunts, cousins. My father was an important government official and could not get away with us. Rebels had come looking for him at the house after dark twice, thrice. I remember our little party climbing one hill after another. Then in the distance someone hears the low thrum of an approaching plane. *"Plane! Plane's coming! Lie down! Lie down!"* While we had no real idea what was happening, much later we learned the Indian government had sent jet fighters to bomb Aizawl, the only time in history that the Indian Air Force was ever used to drop bombs on targets within its own territory.

At that point in time, we all simply crouch low, motionless and breathless with fear on the steep cliff side. I am securely strapped to my grandfather's back. Then I see my mother below momentarily lose her footing and call out to her in panic, *"Ka nu! Ka nu!"*

I remember little else of the before or after of that flight of terror. Just that single traumatic moment suspended in time.

Against the Wind

When the seasons turn and the sticky heat gives way to a nip in the air, and that cool nip dips a notch with autumn rains, my thoughts always go back several years in time to when I was young and life was sweet and simple. Happiness then was sitting in a cosy hostel room, warmed by a heater, and Bob Seger singing about running against the wind while horses clip clop across an icy river...

We were young and strong
but we were running against the wind.

These Mountains I Call Home

Home sweet home. As I get older, I find cliches to be increasingly unerringly true. It was an indescribable feeling the night I woke up in my own bed after a couple of weeks away. Half asleep as I was, I had this unshakeable feeling that this was the loveliest, most wonderful bed I had ever slept in, the most beautiful room I'd ever been in, the most blessed sleep I'd ever slept. Ever.

And it is always a beautiful time of year up here in these mountains. The rain and sticky heat are gone, and in their place comes stealing in what I call the sad soft feel of a year preparing to depart. A precious ambience I've come to associate over the years with oranges, dusty roads, woollen clothes, cold nights, warming your back in the morning sun and ah, Christmas. And all the connotations of the year with its problems and difficulties doing a fast fade, and an anxious excitement for the new year to come in as if all the old year's problems will dissolve away with the last sunset. On the flip side, there's also the implicit realisation that all the year's good times and treasured memories will slide further away in time. Another year gone, another time was.

Time comes, time goes. Seasons change. People come and people go. But these mountains are eternal.

Christy

The phone trills for the umpteenth time that day. Tring, triiing, Triiiiiiinnnnggg. Pi Ziri had placed an ad in a local newspaper for a daily domestic helper a couple of days ago and there have been many callers.

"Hello," she says.

"Hello, I'm calling about your advertisement in Vanglaini." It's a childishly young female voice. Almost breathless.

"Yes, where are you calling from?" Pi Ziri says.

The caller tells her. It sounds a little far away from their locality and she's not sure if the girl will manage to get here every morning at 8.30.

"What's your name and how old are you?" she asks dubiously. The girl sounds like a child. Or a preteen, at best.

"Christy, and I'm 21," she says, surprising Pi Ziri.

They talk further. The girl assures Pi Ziri she has experience working in private homes and names a couple of localities where she's worked before. Pi Ziri gives her their address and asks her to come for a short interview so they can meet and talk face to face. It's normal practice. Pi Ziri had a colleague who had once hired a girl off a phone call but had turned out to be something of a drug addict, to the horror of the family. So Pi Ziki keeps that in mind and is doubly cautious.

When Christy arrives later that evening, Pi Ziri immediately notes she's very slender. Much like her voice, she looks more like a child than a 21 year old. But as they talk, the girl reveals she has a son, a three year old. She had been married but was now separated from her husband who had remarried and the new wife didn't want the boy around. Christy's problem is that she lives with her father and stepmother who's not too keen on the boy either. So she's trying to move out and support herself, and has rented a small room just next to her maternal cousins. She hopes to bring up her son as a single working mother.

Pi Ziri takes a liking to the girl, feeling sympathetic to her problems. She seems reliable and well-mannered, unlike the other candidates who had come by earlier. One had too much make-up on and dressed too flashily, another had picked up her ringing phone and conversed with her caller even as Pi Ziri had sat across her, and another had unsightly paan-stained teeth and reeked of zarda. Pi Ziri had not been impressed by any of them and had mentally marked them all off her list. By comparison, Christy seems like a gift from heaven so Pi Ziri makes a snap decision and tells her she can start work tomorrow and to arrive by 8.30 am, bringing work clothes with her. Christy looks happy and relieved and thanks Pi Ziri, telling her that she will not be late.

Christy keeps her word and arrives at 8.25 am the next morning. She has brought her work clothes, and quickly changes from a simple yellow t-shirt and slightly faded blue jeans into old brown shorts and a black tank top. Pi Ziri sets her to work sweeping the house and swabbing the floors. She works quickly and efficiently with practised ease, clearly used to this sort of work. She is also stronger than she looks, hauling around buckets of water with relative ease. She also turns out to be a natural in the kitchen, preparing the evening meals, and quickly picking up Pi Ziki's style of cooking meat or vegetables.

Pi Ziri's family isn't especially large. Her husband had died several years ago in a road accident. He had been driving the family car enroute to Shillong to visit an ailing relative when a Sumo came from the opposite direction at a terrifying speed and crashed into the car. Pi Ziki's husband and his lone passenger, a young man from their locality, had been instantly killed. Their two daughters are now in their 20s, one employed in a private English medium school and the other a student at Mizoram University. They both leave home early in the morning and get back after 5.30 pm. Pi Ziri needs a daily helper as she is getting on with age, and having recently retired from 27 years of working in various government departments, with her little pension nest egg, she feels entitled to not having to be bogged down with repetitive household chores. Besides she's also a little lonely at home without anyone to talk to all day.

As the days pass into a couple of weeks, all is well until one day as they're having tea Christy mentions that she's having trouble with her son. She had been leaving him with an older cousin who lived next door who had just left a job much like Christy's and wanted to take a break for at least a couple of months. But the family she had worked for had faced a sudden crisis and begged her to return. This left the little boy with no one to take care of him while his mother was at work since the other cousins are all male who also go out to work every day. Pi Ziki is sympathetic but doesn't know what to suggest. Christy begins to arrive in the mornings increasingly late. She says she's trying to find relatives or friends to take care of the boy. One morning she turns up around 10.30 saying she had decided to put the boy in an orphanage and had to meet the Home authorities. They wanted to know details of the child and his family for official documentation.

She tells Pi Ziki, "One of the workers told me there are other people doing the same thing I'm doing. When they sort out their problems and can take care of their child again, they go back and take the child out of the Home." Pi Ziki doesn't know very much about the inner workings of orphanages or Homes, but she does agree that it sounds like an ideal solution for Christy.

While seemingly having made up her mind about the situation, Christy appears distracted and preoccupied. Her work is still satisfactory but Pi Ziki now occasionally has to remind her about certain chores. Such as bringing in the laundry when it rains suddenly or emptying the dustbins at the end of the day. Pi Ziki has to say, "Christy, the laundry! It's raining again!" Or "Did you remember to empty out the trash, dear?" as Christy prepares to change out of her work clothes to go home.

A few days later, she comes in and announces that she had taken her little boy to the Home and left him there. There are other children his age and he had seemed happy to have company. Pi Ziki breathes a secret sigh of relief.

A week later however, the girl doesn't show up. Not at 9, not at 9.30, not even at 10. Pi Ziki calls her on the phone, three/four times. Christy doesn't answer. She doesn't turn up the next day either. Finally on the third day, late in the evening, she calls and says she cannot continue her job. There have been problems at the Home and she has had to take her son out. She has also gone back to live with her father and stepmother, taking the child with her.

Pi Ziki places a new ad in the newspaper. After a couple of days, it is published and her phone rings again.

"Hello," she says.
And it starts all over again.